CLOTTED CREAM ON

Reflections of a Dei

Clotted Cream on the Tonsils

Reflections of a Devon Incomer

Tricia Gerrish

Best wishes

Tricia Gerrish

ORCHARD
PUBLICATIONS

Thank You to:

Mike Allen, of BBC Radio Devon, who gave me the
opportunity to create this series.

Anne McInnes, for kindling the fires of inspiration
– and continuing to fan them.

My husband, Michael, for his support, and for
acting as a 'listening ear'.

First published in Great Britain in 1993

Front cover and illustrations by Brian Steffens

ISBN 0 9519027 9 2

ORCHARD PUBLICATIONS
2 Orchard Close
Chudleigh
Newton Abbot
Devon TQ13 0LR
Tel: (0626) 852714

Typeset by Kestrel Data, Exeter.

Printed and bound in Great Britain by
Short Run Press, Exeter.

First, Catch Your Devonian

We're not Devonians. A couple of incomers, that's what we are. My husband hails from generations of North Somerset stock and I take bets on where I come from. My mother and father were Maid and Man of Kent, and I was born in Bath in Somerset, not the kind you wallow in with half a packet of Radox – I spent every childhood summer in Kent, with grandparents who talked of East Anglia as 'home'. No wonder I'm confused.

'The trouble with Devon is, it's full of Devonians,' we were told by friends and neighbours in Bristol. 'Very nice for holidays, but live there – ooh. They'll call you "my lover", and you'll feel a complete outsider.'

'Do you come from Devon then?' I asked the estate agent in Exmouth. He didn't sound local, but when you're moving to a new area, it's wise to be tactful.

'Devonian? No, not me,' was the response. 'We came here ten years ago – intended to stay six months. That makes me an incomer.'

None of my new neighbours claimed to be natives. Apparently, most of them moved here to retire, in their heyday – the 1970s. They proudly set out gardens with tiny conifers, and with rockeries, dotted with minute alpines. Now, conifers block out the light; alpines have either taken over, or long since perished. Strains of the electric hedge cutter or chain-saw have succeeded the sound of spade on rock-hard clay. A Devon bank, marking the boundary of the bungalows has vanished beneath roads and houses, many of them occupied by incomers.

'What part of Devon are you from?' I asked a colleague in our museum.

'I'm not from Devon – I'm a Cornishman!' he retorted. 'I just retired here from Bristol.' I was tempted to ask if his visa had expired.

1

To me, the Cornish are a race apart. Is it something they put in the pasties, or culture shock from crossing the Tamar do you suppose?

Several times I have been called 'my lover' – in shops, or on buses. The burr in the voice, tonsils coated in generations of clotted cream, is unmistakably Devonian – or so I thought. People who claim to have lived in this town for years then disappoint me, by saying their parents moved here from Hertfordshire, or Bury St Edmunds – so they aren't really Devonian.

Visitors to Devon are quick to claim any connections they have with the county. We get lots of nostalgia trips at our local museum. One lady wrote in the Visitors' Book, horror tinged with secret delight: 'when I find my picture in a museum, I know I'm getting old.' Child of Devon, she is photographed for all to see, resplendent in grammar school gymslip and navy blue hair bows. Both her parents came from old Devon families, which makes her a Devonian – exiled in Milton Keynes.

'I'M NOT A GROCKLE – I LIVE HERE' proclaimed a sticker in the yellow hatchback, parked beside me last week. Live here they may: Devonians they are not. I know a Yorkshire accent when I hear one. The sentiment behind their claim is one lots of us can echo, however.

I have found Devonians – plenty of them. They are generous people: anxious to share their beautiful county with those who want to admire and preserve it. What they won't tolerate are incomers who want to 'improve' it. They know it doesn't need that kind of improvement.

One Devonian friend vividly recalls to me her Grannie's cottage in Sheepwash, as though it were yesterday she visited it as a child. Another recounts tales of cockling in the Exe estuary, and showed me the bench his Grandad always occupied (and often fell off), outside a village pub.

I envy the real Devonians. Imagine tracing your roots back into red sandstone soil, winding hedge-filled lanes, and the miscellany of coves and beaches that make up Devon's coastline. Thatch and longhouses, rolling hills and river valleys – this is the heritage Devonians can claim as their own.

Small wonder city dwellers brave the A30 and M5 bottlenecks year after year. They carry back with them, not only fading sunburn – or rust, depending on the weather – but the flavour of a different world. And if they still cling to their illusions that all Devonians chew straws, and only think when there is an 'r' in the month – what of it? Devonians know – and we incomers soon learn – they're probably the most intelligent bunch in England. After all, they choose to belong to Devon.

50p For The Meter

'Well, we're in,' said my ever-loving. He deposited our microwave on the last visible area of carpet.

All the lights went out. I had a torch somewhere – but where? We groped our way downstairs to the meters, which were suspended where a seven foot man could reach them – if he stood on tiptoe.

'Have you got the bag of 50 pences?'

'No, you had it.' I had packed it. We groped in bag and pockets, and found two coins. Just as well, we put the first into the economy seven box. You don't get much light from storage heaters.

Money for meters – and for the launderette, became an obsession during the next three months. We were renting an off-season holiday home in Exmouth – where we intended to settle. After years of city life, our delight in this estuary town grew daily. Fresh air, sandy beaches – peace and quiet. Who cared that we owned nothing at present, apart from what filled the largest bedroom, the contents of several storage pallets in Bristol, and my red Fiat.

At least once a week, I entered the bank, bag swinging jauntily from my left shoulder. I staggered out with a distinct list to port. Everything was electric: heaters, water, fire, lights, TV, cooker, microwave . . . the list was endless. With two starving meters to choose from, a kitchen chair which served as a stool grew quite dizzy.

We arrived into an unusually cold autumn and winter, for Exmouth. I was just another unemployment statistic, with no library or office to warm up in during the day. Hall, toilet and kitchen in our holiday home resembled ice boxes; I became adept at sprinting through the hall, into kitchen or loo, and out again. We saved the heat for mealtimes, leaving the oven door open. Even so, it cost a fortune in 50 pence pieces, since the oven thermostat only worked on odd-numbered days, usually for a maximum of thirty minutes. Anything

requiring more than half an hour's cooking time either remained half raw, or burned to a cinder. Was I glad we had brought our microwave!

We found a bungalow to purchase; I spent a great deal of time – and money – in the nearest public 'phone box. After a week or so it too developed a fit of the sulks. Every time the solicitor or building society answered, it cut me off and took my money. I doubled my visits to the bank, pleading for more bags of change.

There were house rules, given to us in writing on arrival. One of them forbade us: 'to park across the front of the house. This must be kept clear at all times.' At four thirty one afternoon, the lounge grew dark without warning. A small, flat-bed lorry was blocking our 'keep clear' area – and the light. Four men jumped out, scraped half a ton of mud from their boots against the house wall, and vanished noisily into the other half of our pair of semis. We had neighbours.

I've never met such a load of fidgets. The front door slammed every ten minutes or so throughout each evening. Each man left and returned, separately, several times. Faces changed weekly: so did their vehicles. For a month or so, we shared the property with a JCB, with which its owner churned up the front grass every night.

Thursday night was 'let's get pickled and serenade the neighbours' night. It must have been payday. Most Fridays they went home. By 5.30 p.m. the cars and lorries vanished, and blessed peace descended – until Sunday evening.

During the week before Christmas, all but one – by then they had multiplied to six – went out to celebrate. Somebody had stayed at home: the television was clearly audible. At about 11.30, I was catapulted from my bed by shouts, and repeated batterings on their knocker. The home-lover had either fallen asleep in his chair, or retired to bed.

His mates hollered, beat on the windows and kicked the doors. All to no avail. 'They might have a few spare beds next door,' I heard one say. 'Le's gie 'em a knockup.' They knew who lived there – we were the first port of call when they needed to feed their slot meter. I cowered under the sheets.

A discussion followed, punctuated by schoolboy guffaws, and some choice four letter words. Sounds of splintering wood, and a loud cheer, were succeeded by thuds and grunts, as several inebriated men climbed

7

into the house. A loud clang announced they were using something as a ladder.

Next morning dawned: cold and clear. I couldn't resist watching the sad procession of pipe layers. Heads down, and shoulders hunched, they climbed oh, so gently, into their truck, and set off, half an hour later than usual.

At the back of the house, a squashed metal dustbin rolled gently in the wind, its music echoing the beat of a window, that had somehow lost its fastening.

Grockles!

'We don't want them here; why don't they stay at home?' muttered my ever-loving. His direct path through the Magnolia Centre had been criss-crossed by lobster-pink wanderers in shorts and sandals. Narrowly escaping the third spade, and having just been backed into by a twin buggy full of squawling toddlers, I had some sympathy with him.

Devon thrives on grockles; our economy depends on them. Are we grateful? Are we coconuts! There are too many of them – or too few. They expect facilities we neither want nor need. Inflatable sumo wrestlers, for example. Grockles have the temerity to tell us what is wrong with our resorts. We know what needs improving: we constantly tell our councillors, through the local press or radio. Devonians don't need 'foreigners' to tell us what we should do with this lovely county of ours.

Didn't you know? It's the grockles who leave all the litter, and attack our innocent local youth outside pubs and clubs. They vandalise the town gardens, just as the Britain in Bloom judges are due, take our car spaces, and park on double yellow lines with impunity. Devonians would never indulge in such activities.

An old fellow we often chatted to on the beach had the right idea.

'We don't generally call this lot grockles.' He jerked his thumb at two Range Rovers, smothered in surfboards, inflatable boats and wind-breaks. They were getting in a tangle, trying to park in a space that would have been tight for a Mini Metro.

'Daft is what we call 'em.'

In our case, we are 'the biters bit'. Until three years ago, we were grockles. Regular visitors it is true, but definitely grockles. We owned a static caravan, sited on the Devon/Dorset border, and we made the most of it.

Did we meander through Devon's lanes, exclaiming at each beautiful vista through gaps in the hedges? Could we possibly have travelled the A3052 at 29 m.p.h., seeking the turning to Branscombe, oblivious of traffic building up behind us? Perish the thought: we were far too considerate. Even though we were on holiday, we would never have glared as a frustrated Devonian overtook us on a bend. As for shouting: 'what's the rush, you've got all day' – it couldn't have been us, we were almost residents, after nine years of weekends and holidays spent in the area.

From late June until September, I must allow at least an extra ten minutes to find a parking place in town. My regular spaces have all been discovered: by enterprising grockles, or just other frustrated residents? I prefer to blame the former.

We follow another carload of bobbing sunhats and Bart Simpson caps, trying hard to remember they've got all day – even if we have an appointment in five minutes. It's very hard to keep your cool, as they u-turn in front of us, or stop dead so little Kayleigh can be sick in comfort.

'Too many ice creams' we mutter to each other. 'Flaming grockles – townees without half a brain between them. Why can't they stay at home?'

When visitors stay with us, to enjoy the beaches and other tourist attractions, they are not grockles. Our visitors are the family or friends of residents. We have every right to drive them slowly around the county, stopping at will. If we struggle from a beach car park, laden with chairs, wind-breaks, cool-boxes and other paraphernalia, it is quite natural. Certainly we do not expect amusement, nor comments about 'bringing the kitchen sink.'

We demand the best service in pubs and cafes. After all, we are local, and the hard-pressed summer staff will recognise this. Should a Devonian take the wrong turning while seeking a beauty spot, he has every right to reverse into a nearby driveway. However, when a grockle tries the same, just listen to the Devonian's defence of his neighbour's territory.

'Are you a local?' The man in pale blue shorts asked me. His face looked pink and painful; his wife's matched it perfectly.

'Yes,' I said proudly, hoping I could answer the expected query, after only three years in Devon.

12

'Lived here long? Don't know how you stick this dump,' he commented.

'Blackpool's much better, you know. Got a lovely pleasure beach, has Blackpool. This place bores me stupid.' With that, he and spouse walked off, leaving me speechless.

'Well, what can you expect,' I rationalised. 'After all, they're only grockles.'

13

An Exmouth Newcomer In Winter

'We don't get much snow in Exmouth,' said my neighbour. 'Well, not that pitches. The last must have been six years ago.'

'No – t'was eight at least.' Her husband looked up from the pile of leaves he was sweeping.

The argument grew heated; photographs were produced as evidence. In future, I'll be able to tell other incomers 'we had snow here in 1991.' Now we have photographs too, and very splendid our bungalow looks, standing on a thin carpet of white.

There's no difficulty in finding a space along the seafront in winter – except during odd fine weekends, when the boy (and girl) racers weave in and out of Sunday afternoon motorists along Queens Drive. You can take your pick: park with or without sand under the wheels.

I'm amazed there's any sand left on the beach. It drifts around the base of our Jubilee Clock Tower, and climbs to the top of a nearby wall. Along Queens Drive, ruts of compacted sand develop: booby traps for unwary motorists. They slither from rut to rut, as if on ice.

After high winds, a JCB patiently collects the erring sand, piling it back on the beach in massive sandcastles. My grandsons whoop and slide: kings of a castle higher than even Grandad could dig. Their wellingtons and padded anoraks fill with fine grains, which sneak into the nooks and crannies of my car. I shall find them long after half-term holidays have been forgotten.

Walking the beach is a delight. You can stroll unhindered along the tideline, collecting perfect specimens of razor shells, finding whelks' egg cases, and an odd cuttlefish bone lurking amongst the seaweed, and flotsam – or is it jetsam – from humans.

There are dogs too, paying little attention to their owners. Some brave the icy waves, and gambol in and out, salty droplets arcing around them as they shake. They won't be there in summer – banned from May to September on all but two areas of the sands. I wonder: does the Council send someone to clear up after their efforts? Does a man with a giant shovel work under cover of darkness, on the last day of April, or does everything mysteriously vanish overnight, ready for the season?

Hardly a jet- or water-skier to be seen; only the most intrepid of windsurfers sallying forth. Multicoloured triangles, broken only by a dark-suited body, clinging and leaning in the wind, swoop and flop between the dunes and Pole Sands. Left behind on the beach, an unlucky partner or friend huddles, sheltering from a biting wind. Nothing disturbs flocks of wild geese and oyster- catchers, floating or pottering around a rocky outcrop. It won't be like this in July, more's the pity.

Several days have clear blue skies, and views beyond Dawlish to the dark finger of Berry Head. Only the wind, icy cold on face or back, penetrates, if you haven't wrapped up warmly. Seasonal attractions have an abandoned air. Some are in process of renovation: others firmly shuttered against invading sand and the elements. An occasional cafe, windows steamy, is open for trade. A beach hut door creaks in the wind, its owner sawing or painting, anticipating summer, well-wrapped against the cold.

Our favourite walk across Orcombe's High Land, is muddy: better taken in wellingtons, woolly hats pulled down hard over the ears. No larks today, ascending with delirious song, stunning the human eye, in it's search for the winged musician. Only the racketing of a 125 train, streaking between Starcross and Dawlish, breaks the silence.

Sandy Bay is shuttered and empty. Chairs on tables in cafeteria, sheets of newspaper pinned over caravan windows. Rabbits scatter across the turf: no sunburned toddlers or snoozing grandads here in winter. Only a flock of geese, brown and white barred fronts bobbing, samples the bathing water on the beach below.

And the people who work in this huge complex, and in the summer attractions of Exmouth? They must be out there somewhere, in the avenues, drives and streets. Do they hibernate perhaps? Have winter jobs? Go abroad, keeping track of the sun, intending to bring it back here, along with their 'duty frees'.

When our winter visitors fly away from the estuary, winging north, I like to think the summer people will wake refreshed. They will dust off shelves, spruce up paintwork, unearth boxes of sun cream and postcards, and prepare to greet Devon's summer onslaught.

In August, when our town fills with grockles, and seafront parking is impossible, I shall look forward to Devon's autumn tranquillity. To the arrival of flocks of wing-weary northern visitors, heralding for this incomer another Exmouth winter.

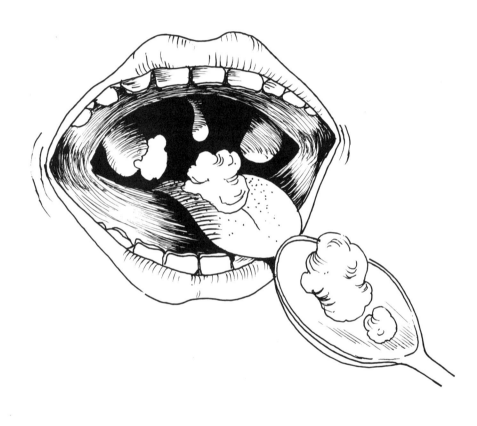

Do Look Us Up

In a state of euphoria, brought on by fixing a date for moving to Devon, we promised all and sundry our new address 'as soon as we have one.' We should have left things that way – but of course, we didn't. When you've lived in an area for years, the challenge of starting again is daunting: the idea of visits and letters from friends and neighbours only too appealing.

'Do look us up,' we told them.

The first Spring rays of sun filtered through our lounge windows, heralding several doorstep arrivals; letters and phone calls began from most of the others.

'Sorry, we're fully booked for Easter . . . and May Day weekend . . . and the Spring Bank Holiday,' we were soon repeating: 'how about July?' I could have done with an ansaphone, and a pre-recorded message.

Doorstep arrivals were hardest to deal with. I personally never visit friends for the day 'just popped down on the off-chance,' with two weekend bags and five changes of outfit in the car, but perhaps I'm backward in these matters.

'We've had such a lovely day – pity to have to drive back – we've nothing special on tomorrow.' Before I can kick him, my ever-loving's hospitable streak emerges.

'There are two beds in the spare room. Won't take a minute to put covers on the duvets. Why don't you stay?'

Word got round in the Bristol and Bath areas: 'We've been down to Exmouth – stayed at Tricia and Mike's bungalow. They were so pleased to see us.' Wagons began rolling: towards the delights of East Devon – and the chance of a cheap weekend. We went out and bought a chest freezer for the garage, to help feed the on-slaught: especially the drop-in variety. Somehow, food bills seemed to have rocketed, and the drinks cabinet looked empty.

My father came for a week in June. I proudly drove him round the area, showing off my local knowledge; fed and watered him with daughterly loving care.

'You made a good move, coming down this way,' he said, as we chauffeured him to the coach station in Exeter. 'Just right for my holidays. I'll be back at the end of September.' And he was! For years, he's been too busy with his bowls to take a holiday. Now, he rings me and says:

'I've just seen Kingsbridge on television. When I come down again, in June, you can take me for the day. Haven't been there for about twenty years.'

One of the infuriating things about having visitors is they all want to see the same attractions. Much though I love the Exe, I could give the commentary on the boat trips up river. Come to think of it, I did, last set of visitors but one. The boatman was heavily engaged in conversation on his 'ship to shore', and I felt very embarrassed, as the one local on board, when people started saying 'what's that tower over there?' It was only when I turned to point to the opposite bank, after explaining Topsham to my friends, I realised I had an avid audience. And the boatman had the nerve to 'pass his hat round', on the way back!

Another disadvantage is the obsession of our visitors with the beaches. We love our beaches: but not at the height of 'grockle season' – and we prefer to visit them as unencumbered as possible.

'Let's have a day on your beach,' they say. 'Can we take a picnic . . . and the sunloungers . . . do you have a wind-break?'

Out with coolbag and box – one is never enough; in go rolls (goodbye large tin of corned beef), tomatoes, fruit pies, apples, bananas, cold drinks. Then we ransack the drawer for beach towels and sun cream, the hall cupboard for boules, swingball and an old rug. The pile on our porch grows higher as we debate whether we need one car or two – it's usually no contest!

A day on the beach – or driving around Dartmoor – or visiting Devon's beauty spots – is pleasant enough. I'm already imagining our return home. Piles of sand in everything, wet towels and costumes, half-eaten rolls – and visitors, waiting expectantly for me to produce a culinary masterpiece, satisfying their Devon- induced appetites. But first, they're 'dying for a cup of tea', and have I got any aprés-sun cream?'

We thought our two bedroomed bungalow would be just right. Big enough, with two living rooms, to turn our convertible sofa into its double bed, when daughter and grandchildren come. That was before we realised you need a booking system, and a deep pocket, to cope with people you've almost forgotten existed – if you're foolish enough to choose coastal Devon as your home.

My husband suggests the next time our 'phone rings, and a voice says 'thought we'd book a few days with you next month,' we quote them our 'very reasonable rates', in return. Trouble is, if they call my bluff, I could end up as a seaside landlady. Maybe I should be like one of our neighbours.

'We've only the one bedroom,' he told me: 'I thought I'd save problems with relatives wanting to stay – so I've converted the other into an extra dining room.'

Come to think of it, I rather fancy somewhere quiet for my writing!

It Might Be 3 Miles In Devon, But . . .

'They've got this signpost wrong,' said my ever-loving, reading the distance to Sidmouth, next to a tastefully carved acorn. 'It might be three miles in Devon, but my Somerset feet tell me different. According to that first sign, we've only gone a mile.'

Before we came to Devon, walking was only a holiday occupation. There's something about living here that makes people want to explore; walking its river banks and coastal paths is to become part of the county itself.

I'm married to one of those men – and this type usually is a man – who sees a hill and has to get to the top. If it's there, he wants to climb it. My ideal walks take place on the flat. I can keep going for ever along a relatively level beach; my legs eat up the miles on a river bank. There's nothing wrong with views from the top of anything: vertigo's not a problem. Getting there is my *bête noire*.

'What a view!' I exclaim, pausing after the first few hundred yards of ascent. What I really mean is 'what am I doing climbing a 1 in 4 mountain – again?' Looking at windsurfers below, or caravan sites – or even peering at the horizon – I can stop and get my breath back without losing face.

From West Dorset to the tip of Cornwall: if we've been there, we've climbed it: Golden Cap, Stonebarrow Hill, Peak Hill, Berry Head, St Michaels Mount, Arthur's Castle at Tintagel, the Capstone at Ilfracombe. I get out of breath talking about them. The first time we visited Dartmoor, I was dragged up Haytor – by the longest route, of course.

We also have to reach the end, and the bottom of everything. Never mind the climb back out again: down to the very depths we plunge. I'd rather climb, if I must, on the outward journey, and standing in

23

a Force 8 gale on the end of a harbour is all very fine, if you have enough ballast to withstand the wind. I haven't.

Leisurely walking is my scene, especially around East Devon. Our Guild's walking group has the right idea. We aim to arrive at a friendly hostelry, where someone knows the bar snacks are interesting, by lunchtime. Good appetites are guaranteed by the walk and conversation that has gone before. Some stride out with determination: others walk sensibly, with deference to advancing years. All arrive invigorated by the Devon air (sometimes fresher than we would like).

We've come unstuck occasionally: notably the day we decided to walk up the River Otter. Early morning drizzle rapidly thickened. It waited until we reached halfway, when the prospect of hot coffee and food in Otterton was irresistible, and settled in to a real East Devon downpour.

My friend discovered her trainers leaked; we wrung out her socks at the pub, and they were placed on a radiator to dry. She only remembered their absence when her feet made contact with polished quarry tiles beside the bar. I doubt if she'll forget offering to fetch me a drink in a hurry!

We all climbed Buckland Beacon, to see the Ten Commandments stones. They're quite impressive, if a little weathered nowadays. The view is terrific: better however, when Dartmoor rain isn't about to set in with a vengeance. One of our number discovered at the top she had no film in her camera. (Unfortunate, as she'd already taken – or thought she'd taken – about twenty photographs with it.) It was all downhill from there, in more ways than one!

Later, I peered through a steamed up windscreen, hunting for Buckland in the Moor, and the Church clock with 'My Dear Mother' inscribed on its dial. My companions, except the one with the camera problem, kept repeating: 'this will help our gardens.' We were in the throes of early summer drought at the time. Would you believe it? – as we splashed back up the A38, suddenly there was no more rain. Exmouth hadn't seen a drop.

Last summer, I was invited to walk a local nature reserve. It's not open to the general public: the opportunity was too good to miss. When I met some of my companions I wondered what sort of walk they were expecting. The only pair of hiking boots belonged to the Ranger. We crossed marshy ground on logs, and scrambled up and down banks. The crocodile became longer and longer in the tail; up in its nose we doubted everyone would finish before dark.

My sympathies were entirely with the Ranger, who at one stage felt obliged to offer to carry a collapsed walker on his back. And surely not many walks end, even in Devon, with two of the party being ferried back in a folding wheelchair – by torchlight!

I've found a little gadget to answer my husband's conviction that Devon's miles are elastic. He clips it on his trouser belt, keeps peering at it, and scowling if he doesn't agree with the reading. Now, as he moves, he ticks like Captain Hook's crocodile.

There is one snag: stride pattern. A tiny lever on one side must be clicked into place, according to how far each swing of his legs will carry him. (As he's six foot tall, much further than mine will!) So, if you see a couple, one ticking, walking around any of Devon's beauty spots in single file, do say 'hello'. The chances are, one of them will be me.

Pick Your Own

Farmers didn't encourage 'Pick Your Own' fruit and vegetables, when I was a child, holidaying in Kent. My cousin and I used to lag behind on family walks through the fruit orchards, and pick what we fancied, but that was scrumping. It was amazing what fell into an extended hand, as we wandered between the trees, dodging stinging nettles round our ankles, and wiping grease bands from our clothing.

Devon's 'Pick Your Own' signs acted like a magnet – at least, they did to me. My ever-loving showed no interest whatsoever, when I pointed them out. 'What's the sense?' he said. 'We've come down here to relax, not to crawl around two inches from the ground for a few strawberries.'

At first, I gave in gracefully; in any case, I didn't have enough freezer space to make the effort worthwhile. Then we acquired the chest freezer.

I made a mental list of items I'd like to pick and freeze. Raspberries were top: we'd had our own canes in my Bristol garden, and I loved them. Ditto for runner beans – though they would come later in the year. 'A few broad beans,' I thought: 'enough strawberries to use for trifle bases and summer puddings. And gooseberries . . . and black-currants . . . and courgettes . . .' My list grew longer.

The first 'soft fruit picking now' signs appeared in Devon's hedge-rows, and in the pages of our local paper. I drew large rings around the latter: my husband ignored them.

'I'm at work all week,' he said eventually: 'And we have visitors most weekends – they won't want to go fruit picking.' He was right, of course – nobody did, except me.

Resigned to going it alone, I collected all the plastic bowls and boxes I could find, one fine Thursday morning, and decided to sally forth. My friend and her husband had apparently had the same idea. We collected a fourth enthusiast, and set off for a farm ten miles or so inland.

By now, we had agreed to pick fruit for another two neighbours, whose disabilities prevented them from joining us. They had thoughtfully provided us with containers, the size of which made me wonder how long this expedition was going to take. Perhaps I should have cut a loaf of sandwiches, and borrowed a tea urn.

By general agreement, we started with raspberries. After ten minutes, the male member of our party decided picking these played havoc with his back, and transferred his attention to broad beans, further along the field. The three of us worked our way up and down the canes, which seemed to stretch for miles, mostly up a slope. I began by sampling the wares: one for me, six for the bowl; even raspberries can get sickly, if you eat enough.

We had the usual disasters: insect bites, scratches, and full colanders dropped between the plants. My friend caused a major panic, when she couldn't remember where she'd left all her filled bowls. It would have helped if she'd dumped them at the end of a row, instead of in the middle, especially as one row of raspberry canes looks exactly like another.

Her husband had found a bench in the sun; even broad bean picking had proved too much, and he'd decided on a quick siesta. Our other neighbour took pity on him, and began wending her way between broad bean plants, while friend and I set off for the strawberry field.

If the raspberry canes were growing on a slope, their strawberries were on the side of a mountain. Experienced pickers would surely have chosen to get these first. They were a little past their best, so we had to be selective – and we were only two pairs of hands, picking for five groups of people. How H. E. Bates' Larkin family had the energy left to enjoy life so much, after spending days in strawberry and hop fields, I'll never know. Still, in fiction you can idealise anything: I'm guilty of it myself.

Three and a half hours after starting, we were facing our collective moments of truth on the scales – and realising how much work we still had to come: sorting, cleaning and bagging, not to mention jam-making or blanching. Our purses could just about raise enough for a thirst-quenching shandy each on the way home.

The final seal was set on our expedition, when we tried to load ourselves and all the produce into the car. Fruit and veg. overflowed its boot, smothering two hot and dishevilled unfortunates in the back seat – I was one of them! Perhaps we should have resisted the sack of new potatoes (ready dug), and six lettuces, that looked so tempting – and cheap.

I ignored Devon's 'Pick Your Own' notices for the rest of that summer, only succumbing to temptation when blackberries taunted me from the hedgerows, in early September.

'Shall we go over to the orchard and buy some apples to go with these?' asked my husband, tongue in cheek. 'Or are you planning another session of "Pick Your Own"?'

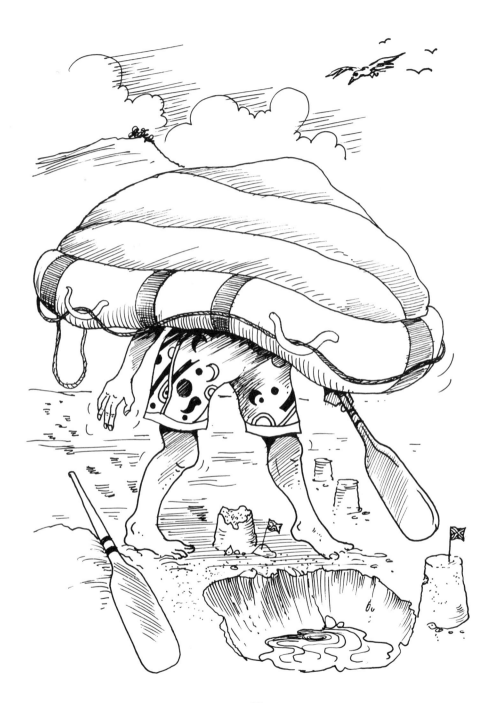

Once More Onto The Beach . . .

I've always loved beaches. Don't mind whether they're sand, shingle, or a mixture of both. My childhood summers were spent on one, very special beach in Kent: swimming, digging, or hunting for shells and marine life.

If you want to hear the British at their best, try lying on a Devon beach. Go alone, stretch out on your sun lounger, eyes closed. It makes no difference whether you recline 'sunny side up' or face down – the acoustics are just as good. Sound seems to carry better beside the sea. It doesn't disperse in the fresh air like you'd expect. I've stood on the High Land of Orcombe many times listening to an Intercity 125 racketing down past Powderham Castle.

Within minutes there'll be a middle aged couple close by, continuing the argument they began in the covered market. She's reminding him of every mistake he's made in the last twenty years. He says they should have gone to Bournemouth –

'Got more to do in Bournemouth, and the beer's better.'

As you grow bored with their cross-talk, the inevitable family gathering arrives. It's worth opening your eyes to conduct an inventory: three cardboard boxes of food, and a coolbag or two, assorted sunbeds and folding chairs, a wind-break, plus three inflatable boats. These are already blown up, and carried over the head and shoulders. The kids will have a pair of oars apiece, guaranteed to trip someone up on the way down the beach. There's sure to be a sun parasol or two, plastic carrier bags, and possibly even a couple of surfboards.

With two miles of sand to choose from, they'll stand in a huddle close by, and argue the toss for ten minutes. Meanwhile, their children run up and down the beach, stripping off garments as they go. At this point, it's very important to have your eyes open, to glare at them,

31

daring them to sit where you feel sure they're about to – one foot away from you!

It doesn't always work: a few large spots you can scratch, or pretending to fight off a swarm of flies might help. Oh – and this crew generally have a loose dog or two with them, even though there's a sign just above the beach, saying NO DOGS ON THIS BEACH 1st MAY – 30th SEPTEMBER. Challenge them, and you'll hear some very enlightening four letter words.

Wherever this party settles, they will be well within earshot. Someone is always yelling. At least one mother will be threatening to: 'get back in the car and go home this minute' repeatedly – for the next three hours. If they can despatch the men and children to sea in the inflatables, the women will keep you entertained with a non-stop flow of 'who's run off with whom,' and other juicy scandal, running down any friend who made the mistake of not being here.

Two women arrive, carrying bakers' bags full of lunch. Their conversation always falls into a pattern. One has everything under control. She never burns – always tans easily. She can 'eat anything.' This means not putting on pounds at the mere sight of an iced bun, like the rest of us. Should she happen to be well covered – not fat, perish the thought – then she will produce medical evidence that dieting is bad for you. Her holiday is always arranged, for somewhere original, and she's sure to be wearing the right clothes for the prevailing weather.

She also knows her rights, and doesn't hesitate to defend them. You know all this, she bores you silly telling her friend so. The friend presumably is none of these things, or has none of them. She's usually admiring, agreeing, and you want to shake her!

When they depart, they'll be replaced by another duo: male, by their voices. A sly peep reveals they're in jeans, or blue overalls.

'Should have brought the rods.' Are the drains in Exmouth that bad, do you suppose?

'Just off those rocks round the bend's the best place' – an expert, obviously.

'Shouldn't we be at that job in Exeter Road?' His mate's got a conscience.

'We got delayed on the last one, didn't we? Caught three or four, last time I was working this way.' Just hope he means he went fishing. It's interesting to speculate though.

Take a quick glance at my watch: on duty in the museum at 2.15. Sit up, collect belongings together, and leave the beach. Beside his open car door, on the promenade, sits a man on a folding chair. He's making phone calls, arranging deals, whilst sunbathing – wearing shorts and very little else. Let's hope they don't improve the range of car phones too much. Our beaches will become full of workaholics, or of enterprising sun-worshippers, boring dedicated sunbed listeners, like me, with their business trivia.

34

Viva Carnival!

'You'll come in the carnival procession, won't you?' said my energetic friend and neighbour.

'Why not?' I responded. 'Haven't been in a carnival since the 1950s. We used to hold one every Whit week, in aid of our local Church.'

Within seven days, my body had been canvassed by three different organisations. It seems they take carnival seriously in Devon. My choice lay between French impressions, Edwardian street traders, and an unspecified entry, promoting natural health, on the back of a small builders truck.

I should have taken the last: at least it offered transport. Under pressure, I agreed to the first offer; then someone told me the route: down Maer Lane, along the seafront, through town, finishing near Holy Trinity Church.

'That must be two miles at least,' I commented.

'More like three – and that doesn't take account of the extra distance you'll cover collecting,' they said. It doesn't include the extra weight you'll be carrying by the finish either – but I'm rushing ahead of myself.

Being a newcomer, all the interesting and exotic roles had been taken by the time my turn came.

'You could be a French artist,' suggested some clever clogs.

'Well, I'm not going as Toulouse-Lautrec. Three miles on my knees is out of the question. I'll be Two L'eaus Loo Trek if you like.' I thought it was a rather clever play on words – nobody found it funny except me.

We posed in friend's garden for neighbouring cameras: the artist, and a very seductive French tart, complete with slit skirt, garter and cigarette holder. Her garter proved very useful when collecting – we offered spectators the chance to twang it: if they paid up first.

Cyprus Road was in chaos, from which order was suddenly

produced, when the judges appeared. We found ourselves trapped between a Mardi Gras style entry, with whistles, fire-eaters, drums and dancers, and a group of bucolic farmers. Once we had been judged 'highly commended', we pinned the card to our French tart's back, as an added incentive for collecting, and headed for the front of the procession.

'We'll get more money near the front,' experienced revellers told me.

We picked a comparatively peaceful spot, formed up behind our banner, and set off along Queen's Drive. Several people had told me the disadvantage of being in the procession was how little you see of the rest of it. They were wrong.

The French tart and I became so involved in collecting, and in chatting to watching crowds, that floats, queens, bands and majorettes all passed us by. I remember hearing snatches of their music, and getting a cold water bath from some sadistic firemen. A young punk on a unicycle rode across in front of us from time to time, only to vanish for half a mile, and re-appear behind us again.

Our tins weighed a ton, as we rounded the Strand. Feet no longer belonged to us. That was my first carnival experience in Devon.

In year two, our entry was a last minute decision. Forward planning, with a flat-bed lorry in mind, came to nothing. We were shamed into entering by the Guild's founder members. A suggestion of lack of stamina, not to say moral fibre, in the new generation, was enough to goad us into 'Singing in the Rain'. I hoped it wouldn't be prophetic; at least we all had huge striped umbrellas under which to shelter.

This time we won second prize. Once more we were defeated by the Mardi Gras entry – once again we avoided walking the three miles next to their brand of music.

I had a brainwave regarding our umbrellas. Turned upside down, they made wonderful collecting boxes – and children loved to aim at them. We found it difficult to transfer coins into our tins before umbrellas collapsed under the weight. Mine spilled its contents twice; the second time I shared the spoils with other tail-enders, who stopped to help me pick them up.

'Will you bring your entry to Littleham Carnival, on Wednesday night?' we were asked. Like fools, we said 'yes'.

That was when we discovered it's all up hill to Sandy Bay – and even steeper climbing out of the holiday park. We hitched a lift, on the tailboard of a steel band float, and arrived home with our ears jangling.

I'm thinking of applying to become Carnival Grandmother this year. It has two advantages: you ride on a float, and nobody expects you to carry a collecting tin.

Our procession is too early for East Devon's well known circuit, with floats entered by famous carnival clubs, but the magic is still there for the latest generation of children – of all ages.

As the Mardi Gras brigade might say: 'Viva Carnival!'

They Must Be Quackers!

Our car turned into Louisa Terrace, just above Exmouth beach, followed by my sister's 2CV. Seven adults piled out, blinking in bright mid-morning sunshine. Beyond the gardens, our much-loved seafront stretched before us, under a Cambridge blue sky.

'Which way?' said my nephew – ten paces ahead of the rest of us, as usual.

'Turn right at the bottom, and head towards the Clock Tower,' I called back.

The 'Caroline Finch,' our local lifeboat, rode gently at anchor, a few hundred yards (or whatever it is on water) from the sea's edge. We wandered along, watching children on cycles and roller skates enjoying themselves.

'Sunshine's brought them all out,' muttered my ever-loving.

Five minutes later, the air was filled with the strains of 'Jingle Bells'. A decorated sleigh, lit overall, and complete with Father Christmas, was about to join in the fun. If you live in Exmouth, or its surrounding area, this scene will probably make sense to you. We were about to witness one of East Devon's stranger antics: the Christmas Day Swim.

On the beach, opposite Exmouth's Jubilee Clock, an area of sand had been roped off, from promenade wall to sea. Swimmers of all ages, shapes and sizes waited for the clock's large hand to reach the hour. At a given signal, a seething mass of bodies raced down the beach, and splashed their way into the briny. I say 'raced': more accurately, those at the front raced. Others were forced to savour the anticipation of that moment when ice-cold water hits abdomen, due to sheer volume of numbers. It was an unseasonable fine morning!

For most of the volunteers – or those who had been 'volunteered' – their dip lasted a bare minute, before they returned to thick towels, and the prospect of hot soup in the nearby Deer Leap. Some hardy souls, many from Exmouth's Swimming & Lifesaving Club, reached the 'Caroline Finch', where their attempts to get aboard were vigorously resisted – or were they seeking to add the lifeboat's crew to the swimmers?

'They must be mad down here,' shivered my sister.

I recalled her words in March. We were hanging over a bridge at the time, watching plastic ducks, with numbers painted on them, becoming entwined in undergrowth beside the river Otter. The intention was to race the ducks from Otterton to White Bridges. Budleigh Lions were responsible for this piece of Devon eccentricity – and plenty of idiots, like us, were prepared to watch and listen, as the ducks' progress was relayed along the river bank.

Duck 'owners' anxiously watched and waited, hoping to win the jackpot for their £1 outlay. Lions in wetsuits – human Lions, that is – were wading about, freeing trapped ducks. The first time we watched, it took ages; this year the course was shortened, but a strong wind blowing upstream, and an awkward tide, produced another marathon.

Tides are the enemies of duck racing in East Devon. This famous colony of birds made another appearance for charity, at last year's regatta in Exmouth Docks. I feel sure they were the same flock: I remember the look in 99's eye – or was she 66 in distress?

This time, they were dropped into the Dock entrance, shepherded by canoeists from Exmouth Beach Rescue. The result was the same; they took one look at trawlers, dragon boats, and a flotilla of Seagull dinghies waiting in the Docks, and followed the tide towards the open sea.

Paddles and canoes were used to turn them, creating artificial waves, on which they bobbed aimlessly. Eventually, most of the convoy sailed through the Dock entrance. It became quite exciting, as duck passed duck, only to be seduced sideways, into a dead calm. My duck didn't win – I only hope she found her way back from Dawlish Warren in time to participate in this year's River Otter event.

We get more waterborne antics each year, in Exmouth, from the trawlermen. Officially, it's an annual trawler race; more accurately, it could be described as annual mayhem. The race is incidental to most of its participants. Competitions for best dressed trawler – and Queen of the event, for potential drag artists, together with flour bombs and water cannon, are treated far more seriously. Spectators aren't safe either. It's not wise to be caught in the crossfire.

When enough cans of lager have been emptied, and flour bombs are only soggy memories, the race gets under way. Hoses and water cannons, generally used to clean away fishy unmentionables, spray from every deck; steering across your neighbour's bow is considered fair game.

Visitors to our seafront enjoy a fine sight: trawlers and crabbers from ports in Dorset, Devon and beyond, clear the Warren, and head for the Fairway Marker buoy. Their return to the finishing point reminds me of that flotilla of plastic ducks: some arrive in style, others limp home, looking the worse for wear, to jeers, and the blaring of sirens.

We are eagerly awaiting the dunking of the first bungee jumper, whether by accident or design, into the waters off Exmouth's harbour end. With a little ingenuity, surely one of our local charities will combine ducks and bungee, and provide this Devon incomer with another source of seafront entertainment.